HISTORICALLY

GARRETT MORGAN

by Maria Mas

Text copyright © 2016 Maria Mas. Illustration copyright © 2016 Cesar Gonzalez. All Rights Reserved.

No part of this book may be reproduced, stored or transmitted by any means without the written permission of the author.

ISBN 978-1530104789   10 9 8 7 6 5 4 3 2 1

"If you can be the best, then why not try to be the best?"
- Garrett A. Morgan

CONTENTS

Southern Beginnings
page 1

Ohio
page 5

A New Business
page 11

The Safety Hood
page 13

Stop and Go
page 18

Garrett Historically
page 22

Timeline
page 25

Bibliography
page 26

Chapter 1
SOUTHERN BEGINNINGS

On March 4th 1877, Garrett Augustus Morgan was born in Kentucky, USA. His parents were former slaves who were freed after the 1863 Emancipation Proclamation, a ruling by President Abraham Lincoln that granted freedom to slaves.

Garrett and his family were black, as were most former slaves in the USA at this time. Many former slave owners were angry that slavery had just been banned.
A lot of black people suffered brutal violence, especially in the South where Garrett lived.

Garrett attended school and also worked on his parents' farm.
He dreamed of being successful and making a difference in the world.

As Garrett grew into his teens, he wanted to be independent. He sought a place where he could prosper and be treated equally. So he decided to leave his school and family in Kentucky and move further north.

Chapter 2
OHIO

Garrett arrived in Cincinnati, a city in Ohio, with very little money. He soon found a job as a handyman for a property owner. But Garrett yearned for more.

Eager Garrett wanted to continue learning, so he used the earnings from his job to pay a tutor. Garrett hoped that this would help him succeed.

As time passed teenage Garrett found that black people were also treated badly in Cincinnati, even if they had a good education. Disappointed, Garrett decided to leave Cincinnati.

Garrett moved further north to Cleveland, another city in Ohio. Yet he still struggled to find a job. Few people in Cleveland wanted to employ a black person.

But Garrett was optimistic and he remained hopeful.

Eventually, he was given a job sweeping floors at a sewing machine factory. Garrett worked hard as a sweeper - but he was a very inquisitive young man and was far more interested in the sewing machines that surrounded him.

Garrett was enthusiastic and a quick learner. While at work, he would curiously examine the sewing machines and their many moving parts. Very soon, he had learned to use and fix them.

It was here that Garrett's imaginative talent blossomed.

Garrett's mechanical genius was noticed by the factory owner and soon enough Garrett was asked to become a sewing machine operator. Garrett was the first black sewing machine operator the factory ever had.

Chapter 3
A NEW BUSINESS

Garrett excelled as a sewing machine operator. He spent years saving the money he earned.

When he had collected enough money, he quit his job at the sewing machine factory and opened his own sewing machine repair shop.

Garrett's new business was a great success and he was able to open more shops; this time selling clothing and hair products that he created himself.

Yet Garrett's curiosity still consumed him. He wanted to find solutions to more problems, so he began to consider other inventive ideas.

Chapter 4
THE SAFETY HOOD

Many houses in Cleveland in the early 1900s were made from wood. House fires happened frequently because of this.

Garrett observed that firefighters had no protection from breathing in unsafe smoky air. So, Garrett decided to make a device to try to solve this problem.

Garrett created a hood attached to a tube that had a wet sponge at one end. This sponge would remove smoke and allow cleaner air to enter. Garrett called this device his 'Safety Hood'.

Garrett presented his Safety Hood to fire departments across the USA. He did this by travelling around the country performing demonstrations.

Garrett knew that some fire departments would not want to buy the invention from him, just because he was black.
So, Garrett hired a white actor to pretend to be the inventor during demonstrations of his Safety Hood. Garrett would pretend to be the inventor's lowly assistant.

People were amazed with the Safety Hood and Garrett began to receive orders for his invention.

The biggest demonstration of his Safety Hood was in 1916, when there was an explosion in a tunnel under Lake Erie. Garrett lived nearby and was called to help in the middle of the night. He used his safety hood to rescue several people trapped underground.

But because of racism towards black people at this time, Garrett was not publicly noted as being any part of the rescue. Some newspapers even falsely reported other people as being the rescuers. This disappointed Garrett.

When news spread of the Safety Hood's use in the rescue, Garrett began receiving swarms of orders for his device from fire departments across the USA.

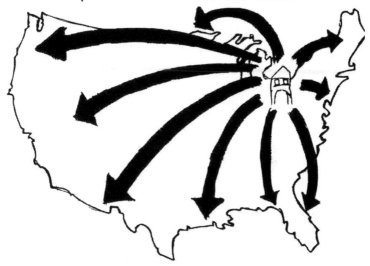

But when buyers discovered that the inventor was black, orders quickly reduced. Garrett felt upset that his invention was now less desired, simply because of his skin color. Despite this, the Safety Hood was another great success for Garrett.
He remained devoted to helping people with his inventions and began to ponder more ideas.

Chapter 5
STOP AND GO

In the 1920's, cars were just becoming popular. Fast-moving cars had to share space on the roads with horse-drawn carriages and accidents would happen regularly.

Garrett's success had enabled him to buy a car of his own. He worried about the safety of the busy roads and decided to create something to prevent more accidents from happening.

Traffic signals already existed at this time but Garrett wanted to improve them.
So, he began to develop his own version of the traffic signal.
Garrett designed his traffic signal on a T-shaped pole with three different signs - 'Stop,' 'Go' and 'All Stop'.

Garrett's traffic signal allowed cars and pedestrians to take turns crossing at intersections.

The traffic signal was another success for Garrett and was used across the country until it was replaced by the traffic light signals that are used in the world today.

Chapter 6
GARRETT HISTORICALLY

In addition to his many inventions, Garrett was dedicated to seeking equality for black people in the USA.

Garrett donated to many black universities to help black people have fair access to a good education.

In the 1920's, black people were not welcome at Country Clubs. So Garrett opened a Country Club for the black community, so that they were also able to do things like horse riding and fishing.

Garrett also felt that most news about black people was negative. So he established 'The Cleveland Call,' a newspaper for the black community that eventually became the 'Cleveland Call and Post' of today.

Garrett Morgan died on 27th August 1963.

Before Garrett died, he was praised by the U.S Government for his traffic signal and was finally noted for his bravery at Lake Eerie.

Throughout his life, Garrett Morgan saved and progressed the lives of many people with his inventions and community work.

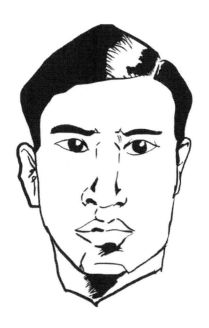

Timeline of Garrett Morgan's Life

1877
Garrett Morgan is Born in Kentucky, USA.

1912
The Titanic sinks in the Atlantic Ocean.

1914
Garrett invents his Safety Hood.

1914
Start of the First World War.

1916
Explosion under Lake Erie.

1920
Garrett launches the Cleveland Call Newspaper.

1923
Garrett creates his Traffic Signal.

1963
Garrett Morgan Dies in Ohio, USA.

Bibliography

Bernstein, Margaret. "INVENTOR GARRETT MORGAN, CLEVELAND'S FIERCE BOOTSTRAPPER." *Teaching Cleveland*. Web. 26 Dec. 2015.

"Garrett Morgan Biography." *Biography.com*. Biography.com, Web. 26 Dec. 2015.

"The Twofold Genius of Garrett Morgan." *Social Studies for Kids*. Web. 26 Dec. 2015.

Oluonye, Mary N. *Garrett Augustus Morgan: Businessman, Inventor, Good Citizen*. Bloomington, IN: AuthorHouse, 2008. Print.

Murphy, Patricia J. *Garrett Morgan: Inventor of the Traffic Light and Gas Mask*. Berkeley Heights, NJ: Enslow, 2004. Print.

"Garrett Augustus Morgan - Affordable Gas Masks." *PBS*. PBS, Web. 26 Dec. 2015

"The Encyclopedia of Cleveland History - WATERWORKS TUNNEL DISASTERS." *The Encyclopedia of Cleveland History*. Web. 26 Dec. 2015

Made in the USA
Lexington, KY
10 February 2017